by Pearl Markovics

Consultant:
Beth Gambro
Reading Specialist
Yorkville, Illinois

Contents

BEARPORT PUBLISHING

New York, New York

Clock to Sock

I see a round **clock**.

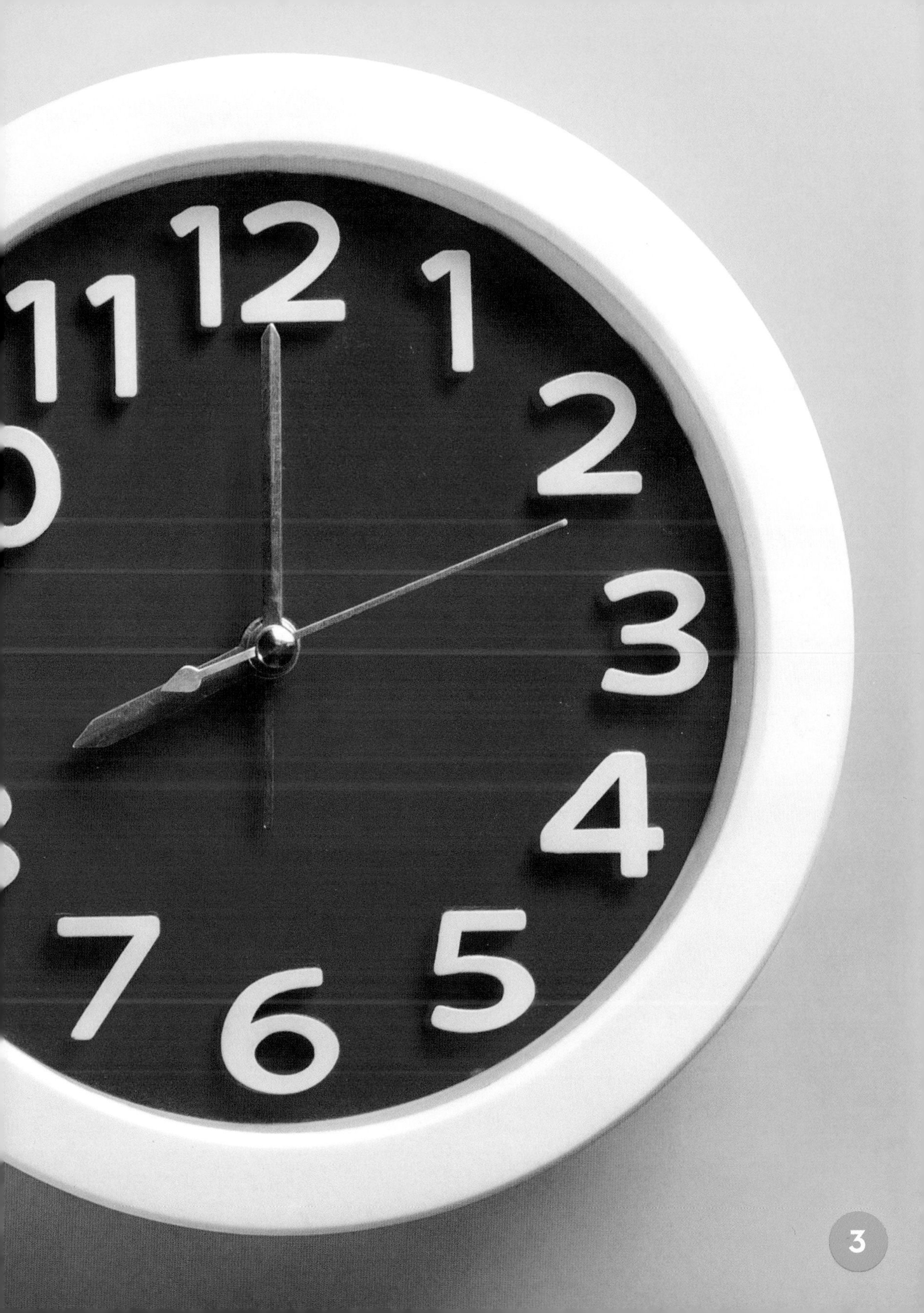
12
1
2
3
4
5
6
7
11

I see a wet **dock**.

I see a gold **lock**.

I see a pretty **frock**.

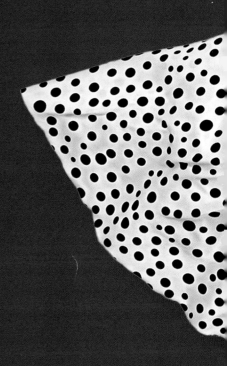

I see a
big **flock**.

I see a
full **crock**.

I see a striped **sock**.

Key Words in the -ock Family

clock

crock

dock

flock

frock

lock

sock

Other **-ock** Words: **block, knock, shock**

Index

About the Author

Pearl Markovics enjoys having fun with words. She especially likes witty wordplay.

Teaching Tips

Before Reading

✔ Introduce rhyming words and the **-ock** word family to readers.

✔ Guide readers on a "picture walk" through the text by asking them to name the things shown.

✔ Discuss book structure by showing children where text will appear consistently on pages. Highlight the supportive pattern of the book.

During Reading

✔ Encourage readers to "read with your finger" and point to each word as it is read. Stop periodically to ask children to point to a specific word in the text.

✔ Reading strategies: When encountering unknown words, prompt readers with encouraging cues such as:

- **Does that word look like a word you already know?**
- **Does it rhyme with another word you have already read?**

After Reading

✔ Write the key words on index cards.

- **Have readers match them to pictures in the book.**

✔ Ask readers to identify their favorite page in the book. Have them read that page aloud.

✔ Choose an **-ock** word. Ask children to pick a word that rhymes with it.

✔ Ask children to create their own rhymes using **-ock** words. Encourage them to use the same pattern found in the book.

Credits: Cover, © Akugasahagy/Shutterstock and © monticello/Shutterstock; 2–3, © Sarawut P/Shutterstock; 4–5, © Grant Morey/Shutterstock; 6–7, © globe_design_studio/Shutterstock; 8–9, © Karkas/Shutterstock; 10–11, © romeovip_md/Shutterstock; 12–13, © clubfoot/iStock; 14–15, © BorisShevchuk/Shutterstock; 16T (L to R), © Sarawut P/Shutterstock, © clubfoot/iStock, © Grant Morey/Shutterstock, and © romeovip_md/Shutterstock; 16B (L to R), © Karkas/Shutterstock, © globe_design_studio/Shutterstock, and © BorisShevchuk/Shutterstock.

Publisher: Kenn Goin   **Senior Editor**: Joyce Tavolacci   **Creative Director**: Spencer Brinker

Library of Congress Cataloging-in-Publication Data: Names: Markovics, Pearl, author. | Gambro, Beth, consultant. Title: Clock to sock / by Pearl Markovics ; consultant: Beth Gambro, Reading Specialist, Yorkville, Illinois. Description: New York, New York : Bearport Publishing, [2020] | Series: Read and rhyme: Level 1 | Includes index. Identifiers: LCCN 2019007354 (print) | LCCN 2019012638 (ebook) | ISBN 9781642805970 (ebook) | ISBN 9781642805437 (library) | ISBN 9781642807028 (pbk.) Subjects: LCSH: Readers (Primary) Classification: LCC PE1119 (ebook) | LCC PE1119 .M28534 2020 (print) | DDC 428.6/2–dc23 LC record available at https://lccn.loc.gov/2019007354

10 9 8 7 6 5 4 3 2 1